101 IDEAS FOR A RAINY DAY

Compiled by Stella Kebby

TREASURE PRESS

First published in Great Britain in 1982 by
The Hamlyn Publishing Group Limited

This edition published in 1989 by
Treasure Press
Michelin House
81 Fulham Road
London SW3 6RB

Reprinted 1990

ISBN 1 85051 396 1

Printed in Portugal

Contents

Things to Do

Quick-thinking Games

Rainy Day Food

Paper and Pencil Games

Introduction

It's a rainy day and you're stuck indoors – alone, with your family or with some friends. It's dismal outside but it's even more dismal inside because there's nothing to do and you are very bored.

No need to be! Here are 101 different ideas to brighten up your rainy days with tricks, games and lots of things to make and do. There are ideas for children on their own, for two or more friends, for whole families and for parties.

You won't need any special materials – lots of the games need nothing at all except players – and the suggestions here will start you thinking of more ideas of your own.

Just a few words of warning – always ask permission before playing any noisy games, doing anything messy or starting to cook. Try not to make a mess but if you do – clear it up!

Tricks and Magic

What better way to brighten up a wet day than with a bit of magic!
All these tricks are very easy to do – you don't really have to be a
magician to make them work. Some are 'trick' tricks, which are
really jokes, but most will leave your audience completely baffled.
Practise a variety of tricks and put on a show.

13

Black magic

This is a 'mind-reading' trick for two people working together. It's good for parties as well as for amazing your friends and family at home and you'll be surprised how long it takes for most people to guess the secret.

One partner goes out of the room and the other asks everyone to name an object in the room. They might choose, for example, the television.

The person outside now comes back in and her partner starts asking her questions like: 'Is it this book?' or, 'Is it my shoe?' The person being questioned will always answer 'No' until, magically, when asked, 'Is it the television?', she will say 'Yes'!

The secret of this trick lies in its name. One of the objects that the questioner suggests should always be something black. (There's always something black in a room, even if it's something quite small, like a watch-strap.) The questioner always suggests a black object *immediately before* suggesting the object actually chosen. So, in this case, when the questioner asks, 'Is it my watch-strap?' (which is black), his partner will know that the next object mentioned will be the right one. So she says 'No' to the watch-strap and 'Yes' to the television!

It's a very simple trick but can be made quite baffling for your audience, particularly if the questioner varies the way in which he asks the questions and uses lots of hand movements like pointing or touching the objects, and if his partner varies the way in which she answers, sometimes answering quickly and sometimes hesitating as if she's thinking hard!

Famous names

You will need

Pencil and paper
A small box

This 'mind-reading' trick is best performed in front of a big group of people. Ask everyone to tell you the name of their favourite film or pop star. As they say the names, so you write each one down on a small piece of paper, fold it up and put it in the box.

Then you ask one person to pick a name out of the box and read it without telling you what it is. After a few seconds of careful thinking you astonish everyone by telling them the name!

The trick is not to let anyone watch too closely as you write down the names. This is because you actually only write *one* name – the first one chosen – over and over again. So all the names in the hat are exactly the same!

Hat trick

You will need

4 or 5 hats
A sweet

Arrange the hats in a line on a table and put the sweet down beside them. Now say that you are going to eat the sweet (being a magician has lots of advantages!) but that if your audience would like to choose one particular hat you can cast a magic spell so that the sweet will re-appear underneath it.

Now you eat the sweet!

Your audience chooses a hat. You say some magic words, pick up the hat – and put it on your head. The sweet is most definitely under the hat but not quite in the way that they may have expected!

Chewing gum choice

You will need

2 sticks of chewing gum

First of all you show your friend one stick of chewing gum and say, 'See if you can guess which hand this is in.' Put your hands behind your back and appear to be shifting the chewing gum about between them. Then bring both closed fists forwards and ask your friend to tap the hand he has chosen. Every time he chooses a hand he is proved wrong! Amazingly, the chewing gum is *always* in the other hand.

The secret of this trick lies in wearing a pair of trousers or a skirt with a tight belt or waistband, concealed by a jersey. Before you start the trick you should tuck one stick of chewing gum into your waistband.

When you first put your hands behind your back, carefully pull out the hidden stick of gum so that you have a stick in each hand.

Whenever your friend taps a hand, *don't* open it but say, 'No, it's in the other hand,' and open *that* one, letting the hand he tapped fall to your side.

Strongman

You will need

A large sheet of paper

This is one of those tricks that makes people seethe with fury when they realise how simple it is!

Take a large piece of paper, give it to a friend and ask him to fold it in half eight times.

The chances are that he'll fold it in half, then in half again, then in half again – still quite easily – but by the time he gets to the sixth fold he'll be having difficulties. Then he'll give up!

Now you take the paper, smooth it out again, and show him how it's done.

To fold the paper in half eight times, all you do is fold it in half, open it out again, fold it in half again, open it out again, and so on, eight times!

Clock caper

You will need

A clock or watch

This is an extremely simple, mathematical trick. Ask your friend to look at a clock face (or a watch) and to pick one of the numbers on the dial without telling you which. Then ask him to draw an imaginary line straight across the face of the clock from his number to the one opposite.

Now he has two numbers. Ask him to subtract the smaller number from the larger one. Then tell him the answer: It's 6!

Why?

Because it's always 6!

If you look at a clock face closely you'll see why.

Knot possible

You will need

A piece of string about 1 metre long

Give a long piece of string to your friend and ask him if he can tie a knot in it without letting go of the two ends (which he must hold one in each hand). He will probably go through all sorts of contortions before he tells you that it can't be done.

But it can!

Put the string down on a table. Fold your arms, pick up one end of the string in each hand, keep hold of the string and unfold your arms.

Numbers from nowhere

This is another 'mind-reading' trick but this time you need a secret partner who will pass on the information to you without anyone else realising she's involved.

First you announce that you have special mind-reading powers and that you will prove it by leaving the room while everyone else decides on a number between one and ten. Then you come in and ask all the people in the room to keep thinking very hard of the number.

You move from person to person, putting your hands on the sides of their heads in a way that suggests you are trying to read their minds. Look very thoughtful as if you are concentrating hard.

After touching everyone in the room, announce the number they have all been thinking of and, unless they suspect you of listening at the door, they will all be astounded!

The trick is very simple. When you come to your secret accomplice, put your fingers on either side of his head at his temples. You've probably never noticed this, but if you clench your teeth you can feel the movement in your temples.

So, if the number is 5, for example, your accomplice should clench his teeth firmly, 5 times. Everyone will be so busy looking at you concentrating that they won't notice the slight jaw movements of your accomplice!

Magic handkerchief

You will need

A large handkerchief

This trick needs a bit of practice before you can show it to anyone, but once you've got the knack, it looks very impressive.

When you do the trick in front of an audience you produce a large handkerchief and say, 'This is a magic handkerchief, it can tie knots in itself!' Wave it about so that everyone can see it, then flip it from the corner, hard, several times until suddenly a knot appears in one corner – by magic!

In fact, you tie the knot in the corner before the audience arrives, but when you wave the handkerchief in front of them you keep your hand over the knot. The last time that you flip the handkerchief you drop the knotted corner and catch it by another corner, so quickly that no one notices you do it.

Weight trick

You will need

A sheet of paper
A weight – a large tin of fruit is ideal

Put the paper on a table and place the weight on top of it, in the middle of the sheet.

Ask your friend to remove the paper without touching the weight. Your friend may consider trying to pull the paper very fast from under the weight but it won't work. Eventually he's sure to give up.

Then you show him how it's done! You take the edge of paper nearest you and carefully roll it up. As you keep rolling so the paper will slide out from under the weight, leaving the weight still standing on the table.

(By the way – don't do this trick on a table which will be spoilt if the tin falls over and marks it. Put a thick cloth over the table first or use an old table.)

Invisible writing

You will need

A fountain pen with a clean nib
Half a fresh lemon
A cup
A sheet of writing paper

This is a good way to send extra-specially secret messages – but make sure the person getting them knows how to make the writing appear!

First squeeze the juice from the lemon into the cup. Then dip your pen nib into the lemon juice and use it like ink to write your secret message on the paper.

Your message will be quite invisible until it is made to appear, as if by magic, by holding the paper over a warm radiator or table lamp. It is heat which makes the words appear.

Guess the card

You will need

A pack of cards

Offer your friend a pack of cards, face down. Ask her to choose one and look at it and then put it back without showing it to you. After she has done this, you study the cards carefully and, after a bit of thought, tell her which card she chose.

How can you do this? Very easily. Beforehand you must divide the pack into half black and half red cards. When you offer your friend the cards, fan them out so that one half is nearer her. She will then take a card from that end of the fan.

While she is looking at her card, move the fan about in your hands so that when she comes to put the card back, you are offering her the other side of the fan.

This will mean that if she chooses a card from the red half, she will put it back in the black half. You will appear to study the whole pack of cards but of course the one chosen will stand out easily as the only one of its colour.

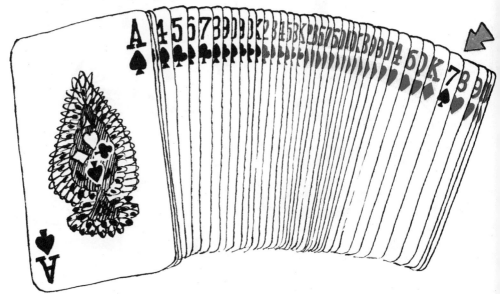

Amazing age-finder

You will need

Paper and pencil

This is an amazing mathematical way of discovering someone's age *and* the month that they were born in.

Give your friend a piece of paper and a pencil and ask him:

1. To write down the number of the month that he was born in. (So if he was born in January it would be 1, February would be 2 and so on up to December, which would be 12.)
2. To multiply this number by 2.
3. Then to add 5.
4. Now to multiply the answer by 50.
5. Then to add his age.
6. And now to take away 250.

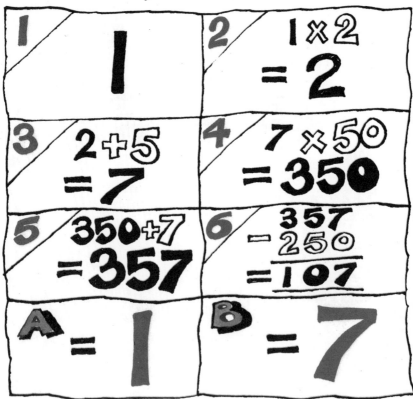

1	1	2	1 × 2 = 2
3	2 + 5 = 7	4	7 × 50 = 350
5	350 + 7 = 357	6	357 − 250 = 107
A	= 1	B	= 7

Now ask him the answer. The last part of the answer tells you his age and the first part tells you the month that he was born in.

If there are two figures the second is his age, the first his birthday month. If there are three figures, the second two are his age and the first his birthday month. And if there are four figures, the second two are his age and the first two are his birthday month.

Left: This chart shows the sums your friend would do if he was born in January and is seven years old.

A very silly trick

You will need

A sheet of paper
Your crayons or felt pens
Scissors

This trick really is very silly but most people like it!

Take a piece of paper and draw a large, funny face on it, but instead of drawing a nose, draw a small circle. Carefully cut out the circle to make a round hole in the middle of the paper.

Turn the paper over and write in large letters around the hole: PUT YOUR THUMB IN HERE AND TURN THE PAPER OVER TO SEE A PICTURE OF YOURSELF.

Now give the paper to an unsuspecting friend, writing side up.

Matchstick puzzle

You will need

12 matchsticks

Arrange the 12 matches in four squares like this.

Now ask your friend if she can change the pattern to leave only three squares, by moving only three of the matches.

Here is the answer so you can practise in advance.

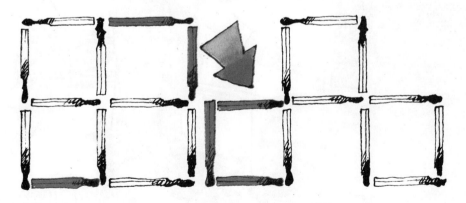

31

Energetic Games

One of the worst things about a really wet day is not being able to run about outside. So here are some very enjoyable ways to work off your surplus energy indoors.

Do remember that these games can be noisy and might involve running all over the house – so ask permission first!

Treasure hunt

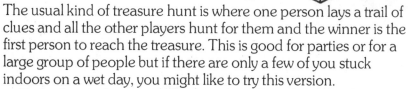

You will need

Paper
Your crayons or felt pens
Sweets

The usual kind of treasure hunt is where one person lays a trail of clues and all the other players hunt for them and the winner is the first person to reach the treasure. This is good for parties or for a large group of people but if there are only a few of you stuck indoors on a wet day, you might like to try this version.

Each player takes some paper and a different coloured pen and writes a certain number of clues. Decide in advance how many clues you are going to have: 10 or 12 is usually about right.

The first clue should lead to the hiding place of the second and

so on, until the last clue leads to the hiding place of the treasure. Each player should have some sweets to hide as 'treasure'.

Try to make the clues a little bit mysterious. For example, don't write, 'Look in the sugar jar,' but, 'The next clue is in such a sweet hiding place!' You may have to wander about the house as you are writing the clues, looking for ideas for hiding places.

Number all the clues as you go along so that the person who follows your trail will be sure he has found the right one in the sequence.

When everyone has written their clues, take turns to go round the house hiding them so that no one sees where you go. Hide all the clues except the first one and remember to hide the treasure.

Then you all swop first clues so that everyone has someone else's trail to follow and off you go. You'll know if you accidentally come across another person's clue because it will be written in the wrong colour.

See who can be first to find their treasure.

Add an action

This can be a very funny game and is as energetic or as peaceful as you make it!

Everybody stands in a circle and the first person begins by doing some action – say waving her right arm.

The next person in the circle copies this action and then adds one of his own. The next player copies *both* actions, in order, and then adds one of *her* own.

This goes on, round and round the circle, until someone forgets the sequence of actions and is out. Everyone else keeps going and the last one left in is the winner.

Do this, do that

One person is the leader and everyone else stands in a line in front of her. The leader then makes some movement – say jumping up and down or patting her head, and says either, 'Do this' or, 'Do that'.

The trick of the game is, that if the leader says, 'Do this' everyone should copy her and anyone who doesn't is out; but if the leader says, 'Do that' *no one* should copy her and anyone who *does* is out.

Once the orders start coming thick and fast it's difficult to remember which you should and shouldn't follow.

When everyone is out, select a new leader – perhaps the last one left in – and start again.

All change!

This is a very boisterous game for five or more players. In fact the more players the better.

Arrange a circle of chairs, enough for all but one of the players, with plenty of room in the middle.

One player is the stationmaster and stands in the middle of the circle. All the other players sit on chairs.

Each player, including the stationmaster, chooses the name of a station for himself and the stationmaster repeats them a few times so that everyone knows all the names. They could be London stations like Paddington, Victoria, Waterloo, Charing Cross and Euston. They could be the names of stations near where you live. Or they could be stations in other countries. Everyone must be quite sure of the name of his or her station before you start.

Then the game begins. The stationmaster shouts out the names of two stations – say, 'Paddington to Charing Cross' or, 'Paris to Rome' and those two people must swop places. But the stationmaster tries to get to one of the chairs before they do. If he succeeds then the person left standing is the new stationmaster. If he fails then he goes back and continues to call out different combinations of stations until he manages to get a seat.

The stationmaster can also call out, 'All Change!' which means that *everyone* must change chairs at once.

The essence of this game is speed and, once it gets going, it can be extremely fast and exciting.

Flip the kipper

You will need

A sheet of paper for each player
A rolled up newspaper for each player
Your crayons or felt pens
Scissors
String
2 heavy books

This is a game that everyone enjoys. It takes a small amount of time to prepare but it's worth it!

First, draw a large, simple, fish shape on a piece of paper and cut it out. Make as many of these 'kippers' as there are players. You can colour and decorate them if you are making them for a special occasion like a party. Otherwise just give them an eye.

Now line up all the kippers at one end of the room and make a 'finishing line' at the other end with a piece of string on the ground. Hold it in place with two books.

Everyone is given a rolled up newspaper or magazine and at the word, 'Go', they must thwack it down behind their kipper to make the kipper race along. The first person to get their kipper past the finishing line is the winner.

Sardines

This game is an old favourite and is always fun to play. It's a bit like a back to front version of hide-and-seek and is best played in a house where there's plenty of room and lots of places to hide.

One person goes off to hide while everyone else stays in one place with their eyes closed and counts to one hundred.

The person who hides should choose a place that's not too small because after the count of one hundred everyone starts to look for her and whenever a player finds her they quietly join her in the hiding place.

At the end of the game everyone is squashed into the hiding place like sardines in a tin, except the last person who is still hunting.

Once the last person finds everyone else the game starts again with the first person to have found the hiding place being the next one to go off and hide.

Things to Make

It's always fun to make something yourself and most of the things suggested here can be made with bits and pieces that you'll already have about the house – so you won't need to go out into the rain to buy anything! And when the rain stops you can carry on playing in the garden.

'Wanted' poster

You will need

A large sheet of paper
A photograph of yourself
Non-toxic glue
Your paint box, felt pens or crayons

You've probably seen those old-fashioned 'wanted' posters that they used to have in the Wild West, so why not make a 'wanted' poster of yourself? It's fun to make and you can put it up on your wall when you have finished.

First, take a large sheet of thick paper – coloured paper looks nice but white will do just as well. Use paints, felt pens or crayons to decorate it with a border round the edges. Then take a dark-coloured crayon and write WANTED in large letters across the top and, just below, your own name in letters almost as big.

Now stick a photograph of yourself underneath – just head and shoulders if possible. Don't be put off if you haven't got a photograph. Draw a picture instead. It may not look exactly like you but you can write 'Artist's Impression' underneath to get round that!

At the side of the photograph write the following list and fill in all your details.

DESCRIPTION
Age:
Height:
Weight:
Colour of Hair:
Colour of Eyes:
Distinguishing Marks:

Underneath you can add your fingerprints, labelling them 'left hand' and 'right hand'. Do this by painting each of your fingers in turn (powder or poster paints are best) and then pressing them on to the paper.

Telephone

You will need

2 empty cocoa tins
  (don't use ordinary tins with sharp edges)
5 or 6 metres of thin string
Hammer and nail

1. Make a hole in the bottom of each tin by hammering a nail through it. If you can't manage this ask a grown-up to help.

2. Make a large knot in one end of the string. Thread the other end through the hole in one of the tins so that the knot ends up inside the tin.

3. Now thread the string into the other tin through the hole in the bottom and secure it on the inside with a knot.

4. Hold one tin to your ear and get a friend to speak softly into the other tin. Stand far apart so the string is taut.

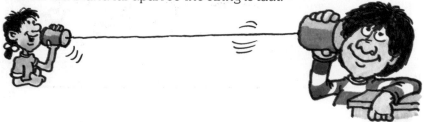

Fruit stone game

You will need

6 large fruit stones (from peaches, plums or prunes)
A biro or felt pen
A large wooden or plastic bowl

This is a traditional game played by North American Indians. It's very simple and fun to play even if you're by yourself.

Use a felt pen or biro to mark each of the fruit stones with a stripe across the middle *on one side only.*

Put the stones in a bowl, toss them up in the air and then catch them again. See how many land striped-side up. Then see if you can beat your own score.

Your own newspaper

You will need

Some large sheets of paper
Biro and felt pens
Stapler

Why not make your own newspaper all about yourself, your friends, and your family?

All you need to do is fold up some large sheets of paper and put them inside each other. (Staple them together if you've got a stapler.)

Now think of a front page headline – it can be anything that's happened recently. 'John Starts New School' perhaps, or 'Mum Scores a Goal'. Then write underneath John's feelings about his new school and what happened on his first day, or interview Mum and ask how she came to score a goal in the family football match – had she been in training long beforehand? Don't forget to draw pictures of the events too!

Add all the other bits of news you can think of to make your paper interesting reading. You could have a fashion page with a sketch of the jeans and shirt your brother bought recently. Put in a recipe – choose your favourite, someone might take the hint and make it for you!

You could write a review of a television programme you've seen recently or recommend a programme that's going to be on soon. Look at a real newspaper for lots more ideas.

Your family and friends will love reading about themselves – they've probably always wanted to see their names in the newspaper!

Chest of drawers

You will need

16 empty matchboxes
16 brass split-pin paper clips
A sheet of wrapping paper
Scissors
Non-toxic glue

You can use this chest of drawers for keeping safe all those little things that get lost easily like stamps, badges and beads. It makes a nice present too.

1 Push a brass split-pin paper clip into the end of the sliding part of each matchbox so that the head of the paper clip looks like a brass knob on a drawer. Flatten the paper clip on the inside of the box.

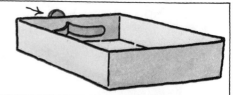

2 Spread glue on the top of one matchbox and stick it to the bottom of another. Keep doing this until you have a pile of four boxes.

3 Make three more piles in the same way. Then glue the sides of each pile together to make your chest of drawers.

GLUE

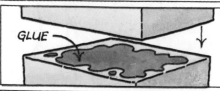

4 Cover the top and sides of the chest of drawers by sticking on pretty wrapping paper, but don't cover the ends of the drawers otherwise they won't open!

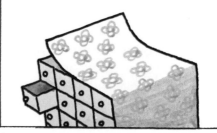

Flip cartoon

You will need

A small note pad
Your crayons or felt pens

This is a very easy way to make a cartoon which really seems to move.

1 Take the first page of a small notepad and draw a simple figure.

2 Then on the second page of the notepad, in exactly the same position on the page, draw the same figure but with a slight difference.

3 Now hold the notepad up so that the picture is facing you. Take hold of the corner of the page, flip the page backwards and forwards and watch your picture move!

Here is another idea for a flip cartoon.

Magic ladder

You will need

2 sheets of newspaper
Sticky tape
Scissors

1 Put two sheets of newspaper down on the table, side by side, and stick the two edges together with sticky tape.

STICKY TAPE

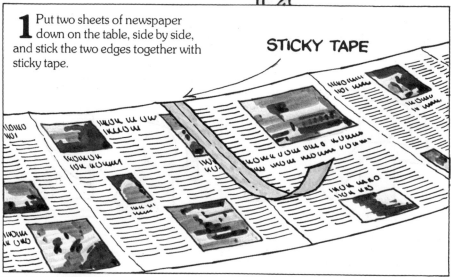

2 Now roll the paper up, starting from one side. Fasten the top and bottom of the roll with sticky tape.

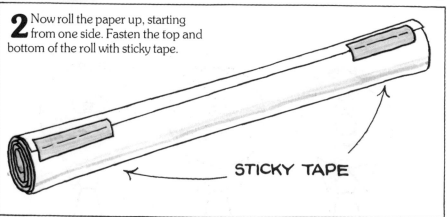

STICKY TAPE

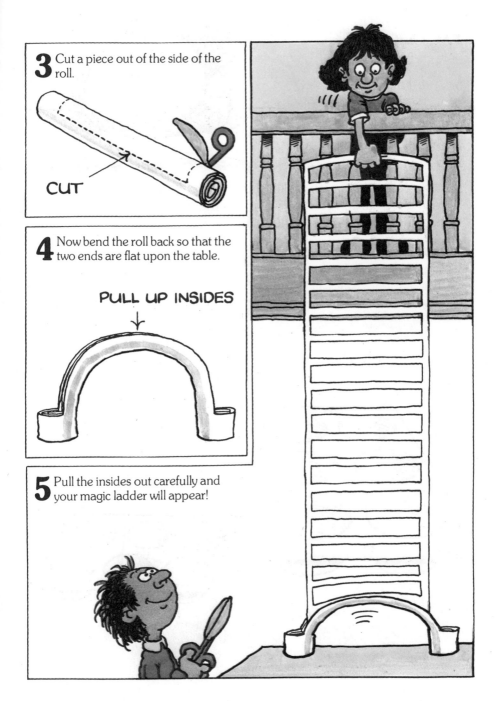

3 Cut a piece out of the side of the roll.

CUT

4 Now bend the roll back so that the two ends are flat upon the table.

PULL UP INSIDES

5 Pull the insides out carefully and your magic ladder will appear!

Bird-feeder

You will need

A plastic egg box
A large needle
String
Bird food

This is a very easy way to make a bird-feeder for the garden. If you haven't got a garden you can still make the feeder but don't add the string – just stand it on a windowsill.

1 Take the bottom half of an egg box and, with a large needle, make a small hole in the middle of each side, near the top edge.

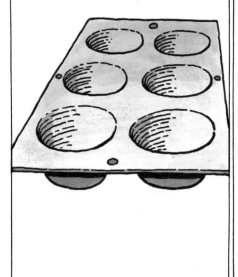

2 Thread a piece of string through each hole, knotting it securely at the end. Pull all four pieces of string together above the box. Join them with a knot.

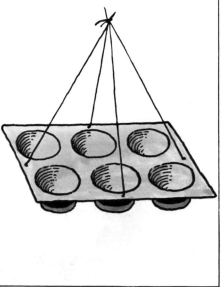

3 Take another piece of string and tie it on to the knot so that it supports the whole box.

4 Fill each section of the egg box with different things that birds like to eat – try breadcrumbs, suet, peanuts or raisins. Put water in one section for the birds to drink.

5 Now tie your bird-feeder to the branch of a tree.

Self-portrait

You will need

Large piece of paper
Felt pen with thick tip

It is *very* difficult to draw a picture of yourself, but here's an easy way. It probably won't end up looking much like you but it's great fun to do!

Hold the piece of paper over your face with one hand and 'trace' your features with a felt tip pen on the other side of the paper.

Of course you won't be able to see what you're doing, you'll have to do it all by touch.

Speedy tortoises

You will need

Thin card
Your crayons or felt pens
Scissors
String

1 Take a piece of card and draw a large tortoise shape on it. Colour it in with crayons or felt pens. Make another tortoise about the same size and shape.

2 Cut out the tortoises and pierce a small hole at each end (front and back) quite near the edge.

3 Thread a long piece of string down through one hole and up through the other. Do this with both tortoises.

4 Tie one end of the string to a table leg about as high up the leg as the tortoise is long. Tie the end of the other string to the other table leg. Your race is now ready to begin.

5 Race the tortoises by sitting on the floor well away from the table. Start off with the tortoise at your end of the string, hold the string taut and twitch it so that the tortoise 'races' along the string. (You may need to practise this a little first.) The first tortoise to get to the table is the winner.

Cotton reel racer

You will need

Cotton reel
Thin cardboard
Scissors
Elastic band
A matchstick
A pencil
Sticky tape

1 Stand the cotton reel on the cardboard and draw round it, making a circle. Cut out the circle just inside the line you have drawn, so the cardboard circle is a little smaller than the end of the cotton reel. Now make a second circle in the same way.

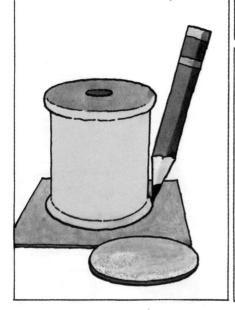

2 Pierce a hole in the centre of each circle using the point of the pencil.

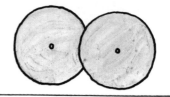

3 Put the cardboard discs on top of each other on one end of the cotton reel. Push the elastic band through from the other end of the reel. Make sure it goes through the cardboard circles too but don't let the elastic band slip through completely.

← **DISCS**

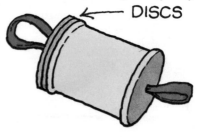

4 Secure it by breaking a matchstick in half and putting the two halves under the loop of the elastic band. Put sticky tape over the top to make quite sure it doesn't slip through.

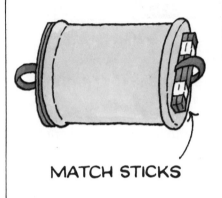

MATCH STICKS

5 Put one end of the pencil into the loop of the elastic band on the other end of the cotton reel and twist it once or twice so that the pencil is held firmly against the cardboard discs.

6 Wind up the racer by turning the pencil round like a propeller – not too many times! Put the racer on the floor and it will speed away!

Personal prints

You will need

Some large sheets of paper
Your paint box and brushes
Old plates you can mix paint on
Newspaper

This is a lovely way of making an unusual picture but it can be *very* messy so ask a grown-up for permission first!

Get yourself prepared by putting on something to cover your clothes and by putting lots of newspaper on the surfaces where you'll be printing. It's a good idea to have some tissues or a cloth and a bowl of water handy too, to clean yourself up between prints.

Mix up your paint and put it on a plate. It can be any colour but it must be nice and thick.

Put the palm of your hand down flat on to the plate and make sure it gets well covered with paint. Lift it off and press it down on to the paper. You can do the same with your other hand and with individual fingerprints too.

You can use your feet as well. This is a little more tricky – be careful not to stamp on the plate and break it! And you may have to paint your foot with a brush to make sure it's well covered, but you'll be left with some very interesting prints.

You can change the colours of the paint as often as you like so long as you wash your hands (or feet) in between each colour. Remember, too, to let one colour dry on the paper before adding another, or the colours will start to run into each other.

Big mouth game

You will need

A large cardboard box
Your paint box, felt pens or crayons
Scissors
Table tennis balls

1. Take a large cardboard box and draw a face on the side, making sure you draw a really big, smiling mouth.
2. Ask a grown-up to help you cut a hole where the mouth is.
3. Decorate your box to make it look really bright and colourful. Stick wool or strips of newspaper on for hair if you like.
4. Now your big mouth ball game is ready to play. Stand well back and try to throw table tennis balls into the mouth.

Family tree

You will need some paper, a pencil and the help of as many relatives and family documents as possible. You don't have to come from a long line of nobility to have a family tree. Even if your ancestors weren't rich or famous you can be sure they were still interesting, and one of the extraordinary things about making a family tree is discovering just how many ancestors you have!

There are several ways of making a family tree. One way is to take your father's family and *his* father's family and only follow the male line. People often do this because they like to know about ancestors with the same surname.

But there's no reason why you shouldn't do the same thing with your mother's family, taking *her* mother, her mother's mother and so on.

The trouble with both these ways is that they take you back into the distant past very quickly. Once you get really interested in tracing your ancestors you may like to start looking them up in public record offices but to begin with it's best to stick to the ones that you can learn about by asking other relations and by looking at family documents and photographs.

See if you can find out the following information:

1. The full names of all the children in your family (including yourself!) and their dates of birth.

2. The full names of your parents and their dates of birth.

3. The full names of your mother's parents and their dates of birth.

4. The full names of your father's parents and their dates of birth.

5. The full names of both of your grandmothers' parents (that's four people in all!) and their dates of birth.

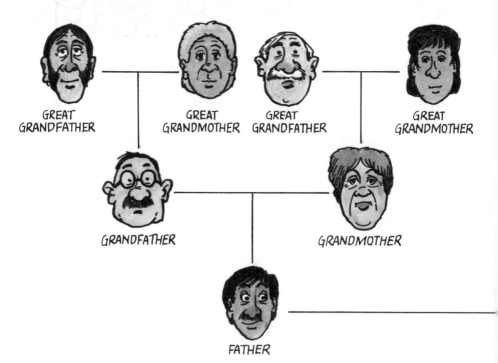

GREAT GRANDFATHER GREAT GRANDMOTHER GREAT GRANDFATHER GREAT GRANDMOTHER

GRANDFATHER GRANDMOTHER

FATHER

6. The full names of both of your grandfathers' parents (again, four people) and their dates of birth.

Then make them into a 'tree' like the one illustrated.
If you can find out all this you should feel quite pleased with yourself because you have the makings of a real family tree and because not many people know this much about their families.
If you want to, you could now fill in your mother's brothers and sisters, your father's brothers and sisters, your grandparents' brothers and sisters and so on.

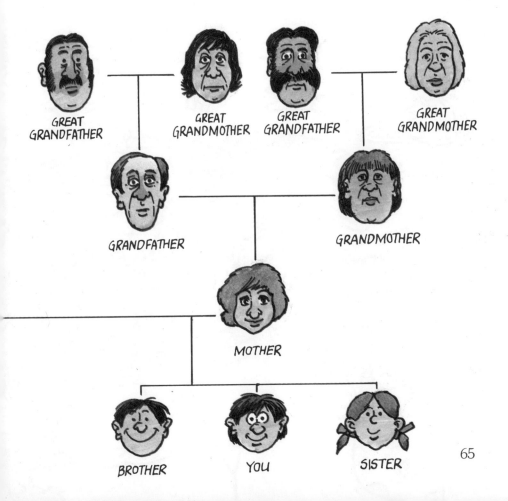

GREAT GRANDFATHER

GREAT GRANDMOTHER

GREAT GRANDFATHER

GREAT GRANDMOTHER

GRANDFATHER

GRANDMOTHER

MOTHER

BROTHER

YOU

SISTER

Laughing and Singing Games

These games will cheer everyone up, even on the most miserable of rainy days. They can be played by any number of people of all ages so they work very well as family games.

Poor Pussy

This game is particularly good for families, as even very little children can play, and the sight of a grown-up crawling about pretending to be a pussy-cat can be very funny!

Everyone sits in a big circle except one player who is the cat. The cat crawls about in the middle of the circle and then goes up to one player who must stroke the cat's head and say, 'Poor Pussy' three times, without laughing. The cat can miaow and purr as much as it likes!

If the player laughs, then he must change places with the cat. If not, then the cat moves on to another player.

Serious announcements

You will need

Paper and pencils

At the beginning of this game each player writes a 'very serious announcement' on a slip of paper.

This should actually be a very silly announcement because the object of the game is to make the announcer laugh. It should be quite short and can be complete nonsense like, 'Scientists have discovered that all cows have twelve legs and wear woolly hats.' Or it could be about one of the players, such as, 'Emma collapsed yesterday after an exhausting hour of homework. Doctors advise complete rest until Christmas.'

If there are only a few players it's best for everyone to write three or four announcements on different slips of paper at the beginning so that there are lots ready to read out.

When all the announcements have been written, they are folded up and put in a pile on the floor. The players then sit in a circle and take turns to pick an announcement from the pile.

The first player begins by saying, 'Here is a Very Serious Announcement' in a very solemn voice. She should then read the announcement she has picked to the other players, still in the same solemn voice. If the announcer laughs, then she is out but the other players can laugh as much as they like!

Everyone takes turns to be the announcer and the last person left at the end of the game is the winner.

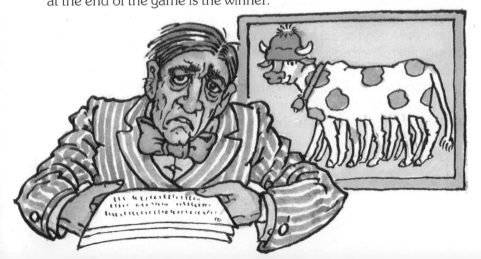

Who's singing?

This game really needs four or more players and can be extremely noisy!

One person goes out of the room and all the others decide on a song to sing. They also decide how many of them are going to sing it. A certain number of the players should keep silent and all the ones who do sing should disguise their voices as much as possible.

The player outside the door has to guess who is singing. If he is wrong then he goes outside the door again and the players inside choose another song and another set of singers. This goes on until the person outside guesses correctly. He then comes in and chooses someone else to go outside.

Sausages

In this game everyone has to answer questions but only one answer is allowed!

One person starts as the questioner and she asks all the other players, in turn, any question she likes. But whatever the question, they must always reply – 'Sausages!'

So the game might go like this:

'Robert, what makes your hair so curly?'

'Sausages!'

'Bridget, what do you see when you look in the mirror?'

'Sausages!'

And no matter how much everyone else is laughing, Robert and Bridget mustn't even smile!

If the player being questioned does laugh or smile then he changes places with the questioner and the game continues.

Face to face

This is a laughing *and* singing game.

Two players stand face to face so that their toes are touching. Another player, who is the leader, thinks of two songs and whispers one title to one of the pair, and a completely different title to the other.

If there are only two people playing, then they can choose a song for themselves. If there are lots of couples playing, the leader should go round and whisper different song titles to everyone.

Then the leader says, 'One, two, three!' and each player starts to sing his own particular song as loudly as possible, despite the fact that his partner is singing something completely different.

The first person in the pair to start laughing is out and his partner has won.

Don't laugh!

For this game, the players divide into two teams and then sit or stand facing each other. The object is to try to make the other team laugh without speaking to them or touching them.

The first team makes horrible faces and noises (but remember no words allowed!) while the other team all try not to laugh. As each member of the team laughs, so they drop out of the line until the last person has been made to laugh.

Then the teams change over and it's the turn of the first team to try to keep a straight face.

Cross-questioning

This game can be very funny, particularly if the detective can remain serious and stern the whole time, looking straight into the eyes of the player he is questioning.

One player is chosen as the detective. All the other players take a partner and stand in a line next to their partner, but leaving a gap between each pair.

The detective then walks slowly up and down the line and stops at any pair he chooses. He looks at one of the pair and asks her a question in a very serious voice – but her partner answers for her!

So the detective may say to one girl, 'Tell me, Louise, what were you doing at six o'clock last night?' and her partner might reply, in as silly a voice as he likes, 'I was disco-dancing with a chimpanzee.'

Louise must try to keep a straight face through all this – and certainly mustn't laugh. If she does, she must change places with the detective. If not, the detective carries on to question someone else.

Sing a line

All the players have a number of 'lives' – say three or five – which are agreed at the beginning.

Everyone sits in a circle and the first person starts by singing the first line of a well-known song. Then she points to one of the other players and that player must continue by singing the second line of the song, and then point to another player for the third line.

This goes on until someone either sings the wrong line or doesn't sing at all. That person loses a 'life' and the last person to have sung a correct line starts up a new song.

When a player loses all her 'lives' she is out of the game and the last player left in is the winner.

Framed!

You will need

*An old picture frame
(or make a frame out of cardboard)
A watch or clock with a second hand*

This is a very silly but very funny game. Everyone sits in a circle while one player holds the frame in front of his face. The other players have one minute in which to make him laugh.

Everyone has a turn at being 'framed' and although it might sound easy, most people can't stop themselves laughing.

Indoor Gardening

Try gardening indoors when it is too wet to dig outside. It's easy to grow plants indoors, so long as you give them plenty of water and light.

Cress eggheads

You will need

An eggshell
An eggcup
Some cottonwool
A packet of cress seeds
A felt pen

Save the shell after you've had a boiled egg for breakfast and put some damp cottonwool into it. Sprinkle in some cress seeds and then draw a face on the side of the shell with a felt pen.

Stand the eggshell in an eggcup on a sunny windowsill. Keep the cottonwool damp and within a few days your 'egghead' will have grown some lovely, edible hair!

79

Sprouting saucers

You will need

The top of a carrot, turnip or pineapple
A saucer

If you have carrots or turnips for dinner, or if you are lucky enough to have a fresh pineapple, don't throw away the tops! Cut one off about three centimetres (one inch) from the end and stand it in a saucer of water on a sunny windowsill.

After a week or so it will start to sprout and, if you keep on adding water to the saucer, you will soon have lots of leaves which will keep growing and looking pretty for some time.

Indoor onions

You will need

An onion
A jam-jar
4 cocktail sticks

This is very interesting because you can watch all the growing stages of the onion, including its roots.

Push four cocktail sticks into the sides of the onion round its middle. Then rest the sticks on the top of a jam-jar so that the onion is suspended, pointed side up, half inside the jar.

Fill the jam-jar with water and leave it on a sunny windowsill.

The onion will take a little while to get started so remember to keep topping up the jar with water. You can keep it growing in the jar for weeks after it has started to sprout.

Orange trees

You will need

Some orange pips
A jam-jar
Some earth
Some stones
A plastic bag

Next time you have an orange save the pips and grow an orange tree.

Put some stones in the bottom of a jam-jar and put a little earth or seed compost on top. Push two or three pips into the soil and cover the jar with a plastic bag. Leave it in a warm place and keep it moist.

When the pips sprout, carefully take them out of the jar and plant them in flower-pots. Keep the pots on a sunny windowsill and your orange trees will make lovely house plants.

Guessing Games

Here is a selection of games that will have you looking, listening, tasting, thinking, acting, remembering – and guessing too!

Squeak, Piggy, squeak!

You will need

A blindfold
A cushion
A chair for every player except one

This game is for four or more players – the more the better. If everyone playing the game is about the same weight then you can play it by sitting on each other's knees instead of using the cushion, but, to prevent anyone from getting squashed, this version might be better!

One player is blindfolded and given a cushion to hold. Enough chairs for everyone else to sit on are arranged in a big circle round the room and the floor is cleared so that there are no obstacles.

The person who is blindfolded should be turned round several times. Everyone else walks around the chairs and then quietly chooses a chair and sits down.

The blindfolded person makes her way towards the chairs, holding the cushion in front of her. Once she finds a chair, she puts her cushion on the occupant's lap and says: 'Squeak, Piggy, squeak!'

The person with the cushion in their lap should then squeak or snort like a pig and the blindfolded player tries to guess who it is.

If she is wrong, she is returned to the middle of the room and the game begins again. If she is right, then the person whose name she has guessed is the next one to be blindfolded.

Coffeepot

This game can be quite puzzling – it can also be quite funny! One player goes out of the room and the others decide on a word that has several different meanings, for example, 'light'. It doesn't matter if the meanings are spelt differently as long as they all sound the same.

They then call in the player from outside who has to guess the word they have chosen. She does this by asking them questions. When the players reply they must somehow use the word they have chosen in their answer, but instead of actually saying it they should say 'coffeepot'.

So if the word was 'light' and the one who was guessing asked, 'What would you like for your birthday?', a player could reply, 'I'd like a nice coffeepot blue dress'. Or, 'I'd like a coffeepot to go by my bed'. Or even, 'I'd like a suitcase, but it would have to be coffeepot'.

Once the player has guessed the word, another player goes outside and a new word is chosen.

Adverbs

One player goes outside the room and the others decide on a particular adverb. (An adverb is a word that describes a verb and it usually ends in -ly. For example: quickly, stupidly, greedily, happily are all adverbs.)

They then call in the person from outside the room and she tries to guess the word they have chosen. She does this by asking each of the players in turn to do some action, 'In the manner of the adverb'. She might say, for example, 'Walk across the room in the manner of the adverb' or, 'Pick up that book in the manner of the adverb'. And if the adverb chosen was 'quickly' the player would dash across the room or snatch up the book.

Once the player has guessed the word, another player goes outside and a new adverb is chosen.

Nursery rhymes

This is a simple form of charades which is suitable for very young children but it can easily be adapted for older children too.

The players divide into two teams. One of the teams goes out of the room and decides on a nursery rhyme. After a quick practice run, they then come back into the room and mime the rhyme to the others. Once the other team has guessed the name of the rhyme, it's their turn to go outside and choose another one.

Older children could mime a scene that would suggest the title of a book, a film or a television programme.

Guess the animal

You will need

Pictures of different animals
Sticky tape

For this game you can cut pictures of animals from magazines or draw them on pieces of paper. One person, perhaps a grown-up, is the leader and she is in charge of all the pictures and shouldn't let the players see them. She sticks a picture on each of the player's backs with sticky tape so that each player 'is' a different animal.

The players ask each other questions to try to find out which animal they are. The questions can only be answered 'Yes' or 'No' and the players are not allowed to ask direct questions like, 'Am I a pig?' or 'Am I a monkey?'. They can only ask questions that will give them a clue, such as, 'Do I eat meat?' or, 'Have I got a long tail?'.

Once a player is sure that he has guessed, he mustn't say anything but must start to act like the animal. The leader will check to make sure he is right, and the game ends with everyone jumping, roaring and crawling and generally behaving like a roomful of animals!

Subtraction

This is a game to test your powers of observation, but don't play it in a room full of precious, breakable ornaments!

First of all, everyone has a good look round the room and tries to remember everything that's there. Then they all go out of the room except one person. That person then takes something away from its place in the room and puts it out of sight.

The other players come back and try to guess what has gone. The first one to guess the missing object is the next to do the subtraction.

What's that taste?

You will need

A collection of different foods
A blindfold

This game involves quite a lot of preparation but is great fun to play.
One person collects tiny amounts of food with very different tastes
like sugar, salt, instant coffee, peanut butter, cheese, chocolate,
banana etc. There should be enough for each player to taste but
only give them a tiny amount otherwise the game will be too easy.

The players wait outside the room and then, one by one, they
come in to be blindfolded, and then be given their samples of food.
They have to try and identify each taste as they go along. The player
who has the most correct 'guesses' is the winner.

What's that noise?

You will need

A pencil and paper for each player

This is a variation of the last game but it has the advantage that everyone can play at once. One person hides behind some kind of screen – a piece of furniture will do – and makes lots of different sound-effects with equipment prepared in advance. Sounds could include: turning the page of a newspaper, clinking a cup on a saucer, cutting paper with scissors, pouring water into a glass etc.

Those listening write down what they think the noises are and compare notes at the end.

Indoor Olympics

Have you ever thought of holding your own 'Indoor Olympics'? It doesn't have to be as energetic as it sounds. And once you've tried out some of these 'Olympic' games you're sure to be able to invent more of your own.

Throwing the discus

You will need

Some paper plates
A newspaper
Your crayons or felt pens

Put an open newspaper down on the floor at one end of the room and draw a 'bull's-eye' circle in the middle of it.

Everyone should stand at a point marked on the other side of the room and take turns to try to get their paper-plate 'discus' on to the paper.

Throw the 'discus' by holding it flat and flicking your wrist so that it skims through the air.

Hurling the javelin

You will need

Some drinking straws
A newspaper
Your crayons or felt pens

If you've been playing 'throw the discus' you can use the same target. Stand on one side of the room and hurl your drinking-straw 'javelins' towards the bull's eye!

95

Swimming race

You will need

A bowl of water
Some corks
Some drinking straws

Each player tries to blow a cork across the bowl of water using a straw. You can all blow at once and see whose cork gets across first, or you can time each person and compare notes afterwards.

Water race

You will need

Glasses of water
Teaspoons

Players divide into pairs and each pair has a glass of water and a teaspoon. One of the pair 'feeds' water to her partner with the teaspoon, being careful not to spill any. The winners are the first to empty their glass.

Stairs marathon

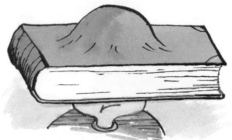

You will need

A flight of stairs
An old but heavy book

This is very simple but can be very tiring! Each player, in turn, is given the book, puts it on her head, and begins climbing up the stairs. The one who climbs the most stairs without dropping the book is the marathon champion.

Tiddlywink high jump

You will need

Some tiddlywinks
A pile of books

It's the tiddlywinks that do the jumping in this game. Make a
platform of books for them to jump on to. Everyone starts from the
same position and takes turns to flip tiddlywinks on to the books.
You can gradually make the pile of books higher to make the game
more difficult.

Tiddlywink long jump

You will need

Some tiddlywinks
A newspaper
A pencil and ruler

Rule lines across the newspaper from side to side. See who can flip
their tiddlywink furthest along the newspaper. You can number the
lines and award marks if you like. Give the lines furthest away from
the start the highest points.

One minute walk

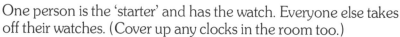

You will need

A watch with a second hand

One person is the 'starter' and has the watch. Everyone else takes off their watches. (Cover up any clocks in the room too.)

The starter lines everyone up on one side of the room and tells them they have exactly sixty seconds to cross it. The players then have to judge for themselves how slowly they must walk to reach the other side of the room in exactly one minute. Walking backwards and sideways are not allowed!

Chinese wrestling

This really is a trial of strength.

Two people lie on the floor facing each other, with their right arms bent so that their elbows are on the ground and their hands point upwards. (If you're left-handed you should play this game with another left-handed person!)

They join hands and, after the count of three, they both try to force the other's hand down on to the ground, whilst keeping their elbows on the floor.

The first person to succeed is the winner.

Elbow marksmanship

You will need

A cardboard box
Some coins

Put the box on the floor and stand a few paces back from it. Mark where you stand so that everyone else stands in the same place. Bend your right arm (if you're right-handed) and put a coin on your elbow. Now try to flick the coin into the box with your elbow.

Each player should try with the same number of coins and the winner is the one to get the most coins in the box.

Patience Games

If you're by yourself on a rainy day these games could be the thing for you. You *do* need patience of course, because they don't usually work first time, but it's fun to keep trying and they *will* work in the end!

Clock patience

You will need

A pack of cards

Shuffle the cards and deal them out one by one in the shape of a clock face, so that you have 12 cards in a circle.

Then put the 13th card in the middle.

Repeat this three times so that you have 13 piles of 4 cards and when you come to deal the last card on to the middle pile, turn it face up.

Suppose this card was the 3 of diamonds, you should put it, face up, underneath the 3 o'clock pile on your clock face. Leave it

sticking out a little so that you can see that it's there. Then pick up the top card from the 3 o'clock pile and put that under it's clock number pile.

An ace would go under the 1 o'clock pile, a jack under the 11 o'clock pile, a queen under the 12 o'clock pile and a king under the pile in the middle.

The object of the game is to have all the cards face upwards in their right piles at the end, but this rarely happens because once you have turned up all the kings you have to stop.

Keep trying though because you're sure to do it in the end!

Patience pairs

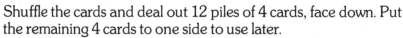

You will need

A pack of cards

Shuffle the cards and deal out 12 piles of 4 cards, face down. Put the remaining 4 cards to one side to use later.

Now turn over the top card on all 12 piles and see if there are any pairs: two fives, for example, or two kings. Take away any pairs that you find and then turn up the cards that were underneath them. Look to see if this means you have some more pairs and if so, take *them* away.

Keep on doing this until you have used all the cards from any pile. When this happens, take one from your spare pile so that you can continue.

The object of the game is to sort all the cards into pairs.

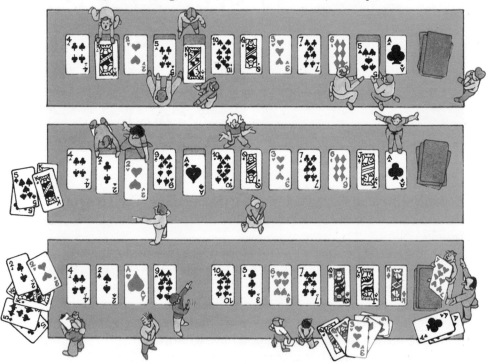

Domino patience

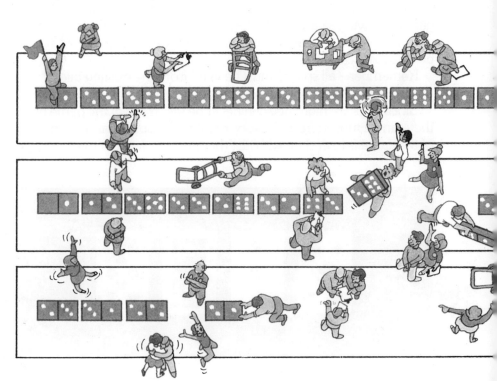

You will need

A set of dominoes

Mix up the dominoes, face down, and then arrange them in a long straight line, end-to-end and still face down.

Now turn them face up, keeping them in the same order.

If any two dominoes, lying end-to-end, have matching numbers on the two touching sides then you can take both dominoes away and push the remaining dominoes together to close up the gap.

Check all along the line for matching dominoes then look to see if closing up the gaps has meant two more dominoes have the same numbers side by side.

The object of the game is to take all the dominoes away from the line in pairs – not easily done!

Idiot's delight

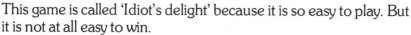

You will need

A pack of cards

This game is called 'Idiot's delight' because it is so easy to play. But it is not at all easy to win.

First, shuffle the cards and then deal four cards in a row, face up. If any of the cards are the same suit, take away the lower one(s), leaving only the highest of that suit. Aces are high in this game – above kings.

Fill in the gap(s) with another card from the pack and if *that* is lower than another in the row of the same suit take that out too.

Continue in this way until you have four cards, none of which you can move. Then deal another four cards on top of the bottom four. Discard wherever possible.

Once you have a pile of two or more cards you can fill in any gaps by moving a card off the top of a pile. This should mean that you can release the card underneath and, with luck, that you might be able to discard it.

Remember – all spaces must be filled from the existing piles if they have two or more cards on, before you deal a new row of cards.

Since aces are high they can never be taken out of the game but they can be moved from the tops of piles into spaces and the object of the game is to end up with just the four aces left in a row.

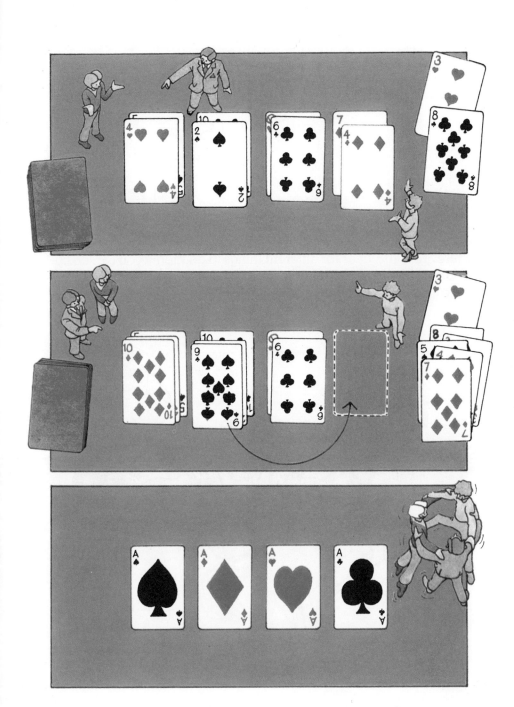

Things to Do

Here are some ideas for different things to do. Some you can do by yourself, some are more fun to do with friends. Either way they are sure to keep you busy on a rainy day.

Dressing-up

Dressing-up is always lots of fun and if you haven't already got a collection of dressing-up clothes you might like to start one.

Any old, unwanted clothes will do, the more peculiar the better, although anything, even what used to be your mother's best party dress, can look peculiar when it's four sizes too big and worn with a funny hat and gumboots!

To complete your dressing-up collection you should have a good assortment of hats, shoes and scarves and even old beads and brooches if you can find some.

When you play dressing-up games, don't only think about clothes. You can make masks too. Paper plates make very good masks if you cut holes for the eyes and thread elastic through small holes in the sides to keep the mask on.

Ask your mother if she has any old make-up you can have for your dressing-up collection. You don't have to use it the same way that she does! You can give yourself horrible scars with lipstick, wrinkles with eyebrow pencil and even cover yourself with spots!

Decorate your plimsolls

You will need

An old pair of plimsolls
2 or 3 pots of enamel paint
   (the sort model-makers use)
A pencil
A paintbrush

Now's your chance to own a really individual pair of shoes – but do ask permission before you begin!

Draw a design out on your plimsolls with a pencil first. You could have stripes, spots, stars, flowers, your initials or just an abstract pattern. Leave some spaces in your design so that the original white colour will be a part of the pattern.

Then start painting, using a fine paintbrush and the enamel paint. Paint carefully so that the results will look really professional.

If you want to use more than one colour paint, then remember to clean your brush thoroughly in between, and wait until the first colour has dried before starting to paint the next one.

Next time you wear your plimsolls you'll be the envy of all your friends!

Start a collection

A rainy day is a good time to start a collection – or at least to think about what you could start collecting!

Lots of people collect postcards – from places they've visited or that have been sent to them by friends and relations. Lots more people collect stamps.

But there are plenty of other things you could collect. Here are some ideas to start you off:

Fruit labels – the little labels that are stuck on to oranges, bananas etc. These come from all round the world and are very easy to find.

Matchboxes and cards of matches – you can often get these free from hotels and restaurants.

Buttons – different shapes, sizes and colours.

Pressed flowers – garden flowers and common wild ones.

Soap – different shapes, sizes and smells!

Sweet wrappers – usual and unusual.

Badges – you can wear your collection of these!

Newspaper headlines – history-making or just funny. Keep these in a scrapbook.

Autographs – start with people you know and then see if you can collect some famous ones.

Tickets – bus tickets, plane tickets, tickets to places of interest, tickets to the cinema – they all make interesting souvenirs.

It is very important to decide how to keep your collection. It's no fun hidden away in a box or drawer. Try and find a way of displaying your collection in your room. Then you can show it off to your friends.

Be a cartoonist!

You will need

Some old newspapers and magazines
A biro or felt pen

This is just the sort of silly game to cheer up you and your friends on a nasty, wet day. All you do is look for photographs in papers or magazines which show scenes of several people together. The best ones are the sort that say: 'Miss So-and-so, pictured here enjoying a joke with Mr and Mrs What-d'you-call-'em'.

Then you imagine what the people in the photographs might *really* be saying (or thinking) and add speech or thought bubbles like the ones in comic cartoons. Once you get started on this it gets funnier and funnier.

Everyday shapes

You will need

Some large sheets of paper
Your paint box, felt pens or crayons
A collection of things to draw round

This is a simple way of making an unusual picture using everyday shapes. Look for things about the house that would make an interesting shape to draw round – scissors are a good example.

Suppose you're starting with a pair of scissors. Put them on your piece of paper and hold them with one hand while you draw carefully round their outline. Then move them to a different part of the paper and draw round them again.

Choose several more objects – perhaps a cup, a fork, some coins, a pastry-cutter, or a wooden spoon – and add their outlines to the pattern. It doesn't matter if they overlap, in fact it looks better if they do.

When you have finished you will have an interesting pattern. Now complete your picture by colouring in the shapes you have made.

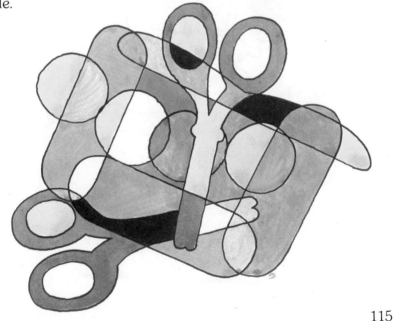

Learn a dance routine

You will need

Some music – from a record, tape or radio

Disco-dancing can be anything from just jigging around to music to following the most complicated dance routines. You can dance alone, with a partner or in a line with lots of other people.

So if you've got some records or tapes – or a radio – to play, why not try inventing your own disco-dance routine?

Practise doing certain steps and movements until you've got them off by heart and then do them in time to the music. You'll think of lots of ideas for your disco-dance movements as you go along, but here are a few ideas to start you off.

You may look rather funny when you're practising your dance but once you get going it can look quite impressive!

Kick one leg forward and clap your hands at the same time.

Click your heels together and stick both arms out sideways in the air.

Touch your knee with your opposite elbow.

Jump with your feet together, turning at the same time.

Scuff your heel along the ground in front of you.

Move your shoulders up and down, one after the other, keeping your elbows by your sides.

Plan your home

You will need

Some paper
A pencil
A ruler
A rubber

Have you ever tried making a plan of a building? You imagine you're looking down on it from above and draw the shapes of the rooms, taking one floor at a time.

Try making a plan of your house. If you live in a flat or a bungalow it will be easier because you'll only have one level to draw. If you live in a house with three storeys it will take a little longer!

Remember to mark all the windows and doors and label every room. If you like you could make a really big plan and show all the main pieces of furniture in the rooms as well.

Once you've had some practice at drawing plans, why not draw a plan of your ideal home – the one where you'd most like to live?

118

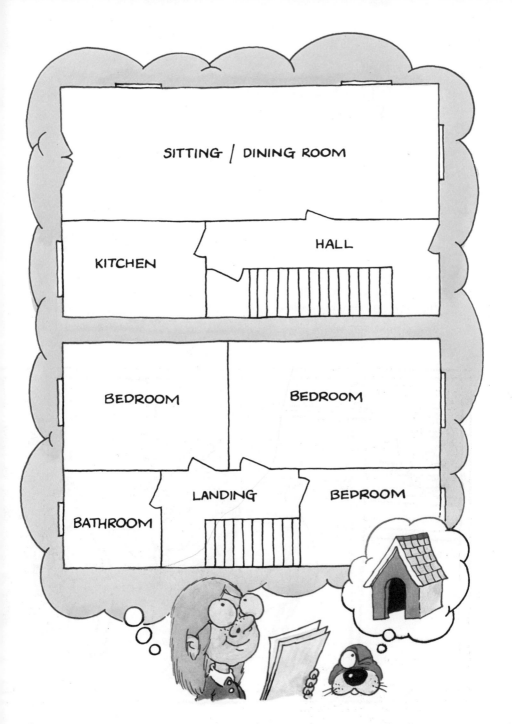

Quick-thinking Games

All you need for these games is to have your wits about you! This means that you can play them on long car journeys, while you're waiting for a bus or whenever you're feeling bored and want to make the time pass quickly.

I love my love

This is an old traditional game that's still great fun to play.

Everyone should sit in a circle and the first player starts with the letter 'A' and says something like this:

'I love my love with an A because he is Admirable.

I hate him with an A because he is Awful.

My love took me to Aldershot and fed me with Apples.

My love's name is Alfred and he lives in Australia.'

The next person does the same but using the letter 'B' and so on round the circle and through the alphabet. It can get quite tricky when you get to letters like 'X' and 'Z' and, in fact, you might like to agree in advance to leave these letters out.

Once you get to the end of the alphabet you start at the beginning again – but no one is allowed to use any words that have already been used. So the second round might start:

'I love my love with an A because she is Attractive.

'I hate her with an A because she is Angry.

My love took me to Amsterdam and fed with Acorns.

My love's name is Amelia and she lives in Argentina.'

Yes and no

This game is good for just two players and is an excellent way to banish boredom.

One person fires a series of simple questions at the other, who has to answer all of them straightaway but without saying 'Yes' or 'No'. (And they mustn't make yes or no-type noises either!)

Once the person answering slips up, the two change places and the one who has been answering takes his turn to ask the questions.

If there are more than two of you playing, then one person should ask everyone else questions. The last person left 'in' (who hasn't said 'Yes' or 'No') will be the new questioner.

Bird, beast, fish

Before you start this game you should decide on a number of 'lives' for each player – say three or five.

Everyone sits in a big circle with one person sitting in the middle. The player in the middle calls out either, 'Bird' or 'Beast' or 'Fish' (whichever she likes) and then points to one person in the circle, who must quickly call out the name of a bird, beast or fish.

For example, if the player in the middle says, 'Bird', the person pointed at might reply, 'Parrot' or 'Eagle' – any bird at all so long as it hasn't already been used in the game.

If the player can think of something within five seconds he changes places with the one in the middle. If not, or if he uses a name already mentioned, then he loses a life and the person in the middle goes on to ask someone else.

When a player loses all his 'lives' he is out of the game and the last questioner left at the end is the winner.

125

The minister's cat

This game is good for a group of players but it can be played just as easily with two or three.

One person starts as the leader. He says, 'The minister's cat is . . .' (then he selects any letter of the alphabet – say G) and continues, 'a G cat' and points at one of the players.

The player selected must then think of a word to describe the cat beginning with the letter chosen. She could say greedy, generous or even green! But it mustn't be a word already used in the game.

The leader continues, choosing different letters and different people to reply, until someone can't think of a word. Then that person is out.

Associations

You really do have to think quickly for this game.

Everyone sits in a circle and the first person begins by saying a word – any word that comes into his head. The next person, going clockwise round the circle, must think of a word that is in some way associated with the first word. For example, if the first word was 'book' the second person might say 'page'. The third person might say 'wedding', the fourth might say 'cake' and so on.

But no one should have too long to think of a word, so after the first word has been called out, everyone should clap – one, two, three, four – and the second person must be ready to say his word after the fourth clap. If he can't think of a word or if the word he chooses doesn't link with the first one (or he can't explain the link to the satisfaction of the rest of the players) then he has lost one of his nine lives.

Rainy Day Food

The nicest thing about cooking is that you can eat the results of your work afterwards! Here are some recipes for things that you might like to make and eat (or drink) on a rainy day.

Take care when cooking and follow these simple rules:
1. *Don't* start to cook without a grown-up nearby to help you.
2. *Don't* touch the oven without permission.
3. *Do* ask a grown-up to turn on the oven and to take dishes in and out for you.
4. *Do* be very careful when using sharp knives.
5. *Do* wipe up any spills as soon as they happen so that you don't slip and fall.
6. *Do* wash your hands before you begin, tie back long hair and wear an apron.
7. *Do* keep your working area as tidy as possible and clear up as you go along.
8. *Do* leave the kitchen clean and tidy.

Pear hedgehogs

You will need

A tin of pear halves
Some flaked almonds
Some currants
A packet of green jelly

1 Stand each pear half on its flat side in a dish.

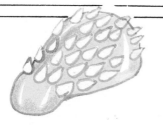

2 Stick almond flakes all over the pears so that the flakes look like the spines of a hedgehog.

3 Add currants for eyes and noses.

4 Ask a grown-up to make up a packet of green jelly. When it has set, chop the jelly into little pieces and spread it over a dish. Sit the hedgehogs on top of the grass!

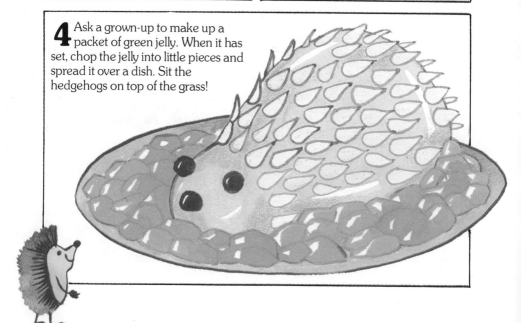

Monster milk

You will need

A glass of milk
A banana
Some flaked almonds
Some small sweets

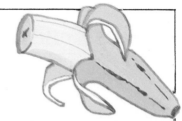

1 Peel the banana and cut off one end.

2 Cut a slit in the other end of the banana for the monster's mouth.

3 Stand the banana in the glass of milk so the 'head' sticks out.

4 Decorate the head with flaked almonds and sweets. Use a red sweet for a tongue.

Next time someone asks for a glass of milk – surprise them with a monster in the glass!

Cheesey notes

You will need

225g (8oz) plain flour
100g (4oz) butter or margarine
85g (3oz) grated cheese
2 eggs
Pinch of salt
Pinch of dry mustard powder

1 Ask a grown-up to set the oven to Gas 6/425°F/220°C.

2

Grease 2 baking trays.

3

Sieve the flour, salt and mustard powder into a bowl.

4 Add the butter or margarine. Use a round-ended knife to cut it into very small pieces, then rub it into the flour using your fingertips, until the mixture looks like fine breadcrumbs.

5 Break the eggs into a small bowl and whisk them with a fork.

6 Add the eggs and the cheese to the flour and butter and gather the mixture together into a large ball. (If it seems too dry add a little milk.)

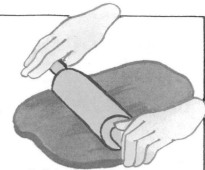

7 Roll the mixture out using a floured rolling pin on a floured board or table top, until it is about six millimetres ($\frac{1}{4}$ inch) thick.

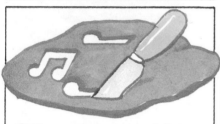

8 Now cut the pastry carefully into note shapes. Lift the notes up gently and put them on the greased trays.

9 Ask a grown-up to put them in the oven for about 8–10 minutes or until golden brown.

10 When a grown-up has taken them out of the oven, leave them to cool on the trays. Keep them in a tin if you don't eat them all straightaway!

Cinnamon toast

You will need

A slice of white bread for each person
Butter
3 tablespoons brown sugar
1 tablespoon cinnamon

1 First make your cinnamon mixture by putting the sugar and the cinnamon into a bowl. Mix well.

2 Ask a grown-up to turn on the grill and make some toast – one piece for each person.

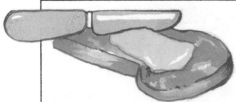

3 Butter the toast and spread the cinnamon mixture over it.

4 Put the toast back under the grill, just for a few seconds, to melt the sugar. Be careful not to burn it.

5 Cut the toast into fingers and eat. You can save any leftover cinnamon mixture in a jar.

Animal sandwiches

If you have some of those pastry cutters shaped like animals, then you can try making animal sandwiches by getting ordinary sandwiches and pressing out shapes with the cutters.

If you haven't got any pastry cutters you can draw a simple shape on a piece of clean white card, put that on top of the sandwich and cut carefully round it with a knife.

The shapes don't have to be animals of course: you could have hearts or circles or even stars.

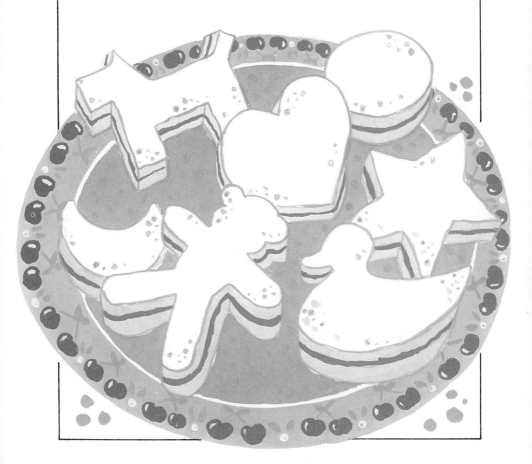

Peppermint creams

You will need

400g (14oz) icing sugar
1 egg white
Lemon juice
Peppermint essence

1 Sieve the icing sugar into a mixing bowl.

2 Separate an egg into yolk and white and put the white into the bowl with the sugar.

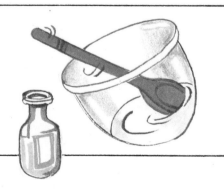

3 Add a few drops of peppermint essence and mix everything together with a wooden spoon.

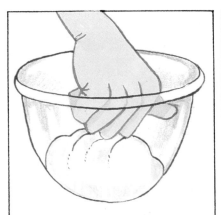

4 Knead the mixture well with your hands. If it is still crumbly add drops of lemon juice until it is soft and bendy.

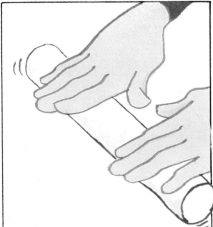

5 Sprinkle some icing sugar on your work surface. Take the mixture out and roll it into a long, fat sausage.

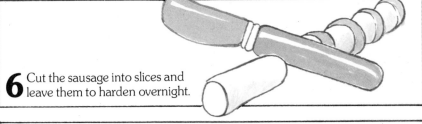

6 Cut the sausage into slices and leave them to harden overnight.

Home-made lemonade

1 Grate the rind from the lemons and put it in a large bowl. Try not to take off a lot of the white pith underneath the peel because this is very bitter.

2 Cut the lemons in half and squeeze out all the juice. Pour the juice in the bowl with the grated peel. Put the sugar in the bowl too.

3 Ask a grown-up to boil the water and pour it into the bowl. Stir well and leave to cool.

4 When the mixture is cool, strain the liquid through a fine sieve or tea-strainer into a large jug. Put the jug in the fridge and chill the lemonade well before serving in glasses with ice-cubes.

Banana milkshake

You will need

1 banana
1 teaspoon honey
1 tablespoon vanilla ice-cream
300ml ($\frac{1}{2}$ pint) milk

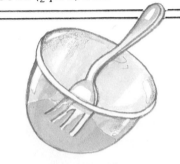

1 Peel the banana and put it in a mixing bowl. Mash it very well with a fork.

2 Mix in the honey and the ice-cream. Mix until smooth.

3 Add the milk and whisk it all up with an egg-whisk. Serve straightaway.

Coconut cakes

You will need
225g (8oz) desiccated coconut
387g (14oz) tin of
condensed milk
Some glacé cherries
A little margarine and flour

1 Ask a grown-up to put the oven on at Gas Mark 4/350°F/180°C.

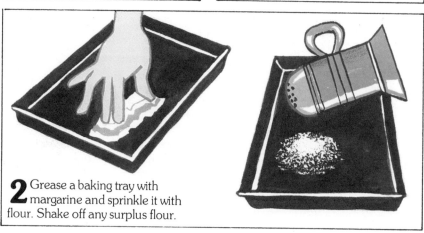

2 Grease a baking tray with margarine and sprinkle it with flour. Shake off any surplus flour.

3 Put the desiccated coconut and condensed milk in a bowl and mix well with a spoon.

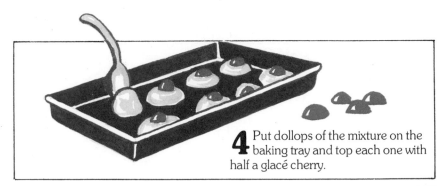

4 Put dollops of the mixture on the baking tray and top each one with half a glacé cherry.

5 Ask a grown-up to put the cakes in the oven and to take them out about 20–30 minutes later when they are golden brown.

6 Use a fish slice to put the cakes on a wire rack to cool.

Bread pudding

You will need

½ loaf white bread
150–300ml (¼–½pint) milk
2 tablespoons of honey
1 teaspoon of mixed spices
100g (4oz) dried fruit
1 egg
A little margarine

1 Ask a grown-up to turn on the oven at Gas Mark 4/350°F/180°C.

2 Grease a small cake tin with a little margarine.

3 Crumble half a loaf of white bread into a mixing bowl. Add enough milk to moisten it thoroughly and leave for about half an hour.

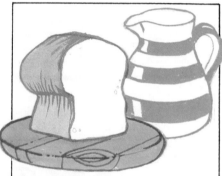

4 Now add two tablespoons of honey to the bread and milk and mix it in well.

5 Add the mixed spices and dried fruit. Mix thoroughly.

6 Break the egg into a separate bowl, beat it thoroughly and then mix that in too.

7 Spoon the mixture into the cake tin.

8 Ask a grown-up to put the cake in the oven for about 30–40 minutes. Put on a wire rack to cool.

9 Eat as a cake or ask to have it with custard for pudding.

Paper and Pencil Games

Everybody likes these games – and they're especially good for a rainy day. They can be played by any number of people, from one or two to a whole party – and all you'll need is a pile of paper and some pencils or pens.

144

145

Animal consequences

This game is fun for any number of players of any age. Each player needs quite a long piece of paper and a pencil. First of all, everyone draws an animal's head. You can draw the head of a real animal or a pretend 'space-monster' one.

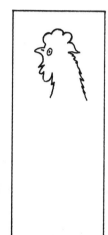

Then everyone folds over the top of their paper, so that the head is hidden, and passes the paper on to their neighbour. Next, everyone draws an animal's body.

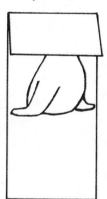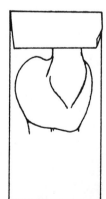

The papers are folded over and passed on and everyone draws some legs. The same thing happens again and this time everyone draws the animal's feet.

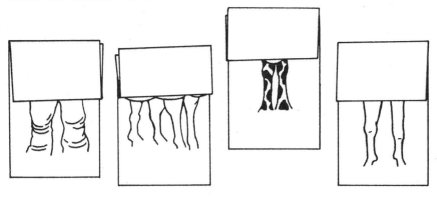

The papers are passed on one more time then opened up. Each player has to think up a name for the strange beast they have in front of them!

Artists

This can be a very funny game and it's good for parties too.

One person is the artist and has paper and a pencil or pen. Another person describes an object in the room for the artist to draw – but she mustn't say what it is or what it's used for. She must simply say what shape it is, what colour it is, what it's made of and so on.

The artist tries to draw the object as the other player describes it. (He's not allowed to look round the room to see what the object might be.)

The results can be quite hilarious. Try blindfolding the artist to make it extra difficult!

Teams

This is a good game to play if you are by yourself.

It is based around the idea of two football teams (but it could be rugby or hockey or any other team game if you prefer). You are selecting two teams to play in a Grand Match. The only trouble is, no real football players are allowed!

The teams might consist of television celebrities versus teachers from your school or pop singers versus people in your family. In fact, any two groups of people that are very different.

You have to write down the names of the two teams and of each person in them, as well as the position that each person will play. Then see if you can decide which team would win!

Codes

Have you ever tried sending messages in a secret code that you've invented yourself? It's quite easy to make up codes and there are countless ways of doing it.

The easiest way to make your own code is to write all the letters of the alphabet, in order, in a line and then write all the letters of the alphabet at random underneath them. Your code might look something like this:

A B C D E F G H I J K L M N O P Q R S T U V W X Y Z
H K V W A J I U B T L S R C Q E M P Y D X Z G N F O

So if you wanted to send a message using this code to say: MEET ME AT FOUR TOMORROW, it would look like this: RAAD RA HD JQXP DQRQPPQG.

Make up a code all of your own but make sure whoever you are sending your message to knows your code!

Categories

Everyone has a piece of paper and a pencil and writes down the
left-hand side of the paper a long list of different 'categories': girl's
name, boy's name, animal, vegetable, flower, country, town, food,
bird etc. You can agree exactly how many categories you want.

Now choose any letter of the alphabet – perhaps by sticking a pin
into the page of a newspaper. Everyone must try and think of
something beginning with that letter to fill every category on their
list. The winner is the first to finish – or the one with the fewest gaps.

152

Alphabet game

This is another version of 'Categories' but in this game you write the whole of the alphabet down the left-hand side of your paper and then players take it in turns to choose a category.

Suppose the first category chosen is 'animals'. Everyone writes down the name of an animal beginning with 'A' then 'B' and so on through the alphabet.

When you have finished animals, another player chooses a different category. This goes on until everyone has had a chance to pick a category. Compare notes at the end of the game and see who has the fewest gaps.

Pass the story

This game is a bit like 'animal consequences'. You don't know what strange creations you will produce!

Everyone has a piece of paper and a pencil and writes down the beginning of a story. It should only be a few lines. For example: 'Once there was an old man who lived in a wooden hut in the mountains.'

But then the person writing should add the beginning of a new sentence and break it off halfway. For example: 'One day, as he was walking up the path to his front door, he saw . . .'

Then she should turn over the top of the paper so that only this last half-sentence can be seen and pass it on to the next player.

The next player must finish off the sentence that he has been given and then go on with the story – as he thinks it should be! He, too, should leave a sentence half-finished at the end and pass this on to the next player.

This game can go on for as long as you like but about five or six turns is usually long enough.

Then everyone reads out the story that they have been handed. The tales are usually quite extraordinary!

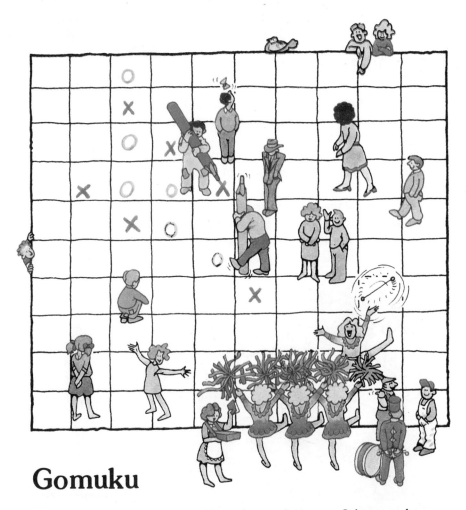

Gomuku

This is a Japanese version of noughts and crosses. Like noughts and crosses it is for two players but the difference is that it can last for hours or minutes, depending on the size of your grid.

To begin with, try playing with a grid of 100 squares – 10 squares across and 10 down. First draw the grid on a piece of paper. Then decide who will draw noughts and who will draw crosses.

Each player takes it in turn to draw a nought or a cross in one of the squares on the grid.

To win the game you must have 5 noughts or crosses in a row, either horizontally, vertically or diagonally. But of course your opponent will try to prevent you from doing this!

Strange sentences

Make sure all the players have a pencil and a piece of paper then ask everyone to call out letters of the alphabet at random. You need about five or six letters.

Everyone should write the letters down, in the order they were called out, at the top of their piece of paper. For example, you might have I H T R S S.

Now you have ten minutes to think of a six-word sentence in which the words begin with those letters in that order.

Your answer could be: 'I hope the rain stops soon.'